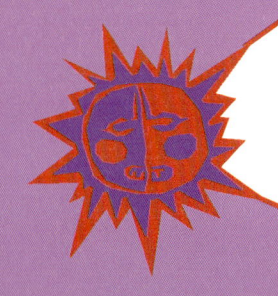

What's Wrong with My Brain?
Kids with Brain Injury

Kids with Special Needs

Seeing with Your Fingers:
Kids with Blindness and Visual Impairment

Listening with Your Eyes:
Kids Who Are Deaf and Hard of Hearing

My Name Is Not Slow:
Kids with Intellectual Disabilities

Sick All the Time: **Kids with Chronic Illness**

Something's Wrong!
Kids with Emotional Disturbance

Speed Racer: **Kids with Attention-Deficit/ Hyperactivity Disorder**

Finding My Voice: **Kids with Speech Impairment**

I Can Do It! **Kids with Physical Challenges**

The Hidden Child: **Kids with Autism**

What's Wrong with My Brain?
Kids with Brain Injury

Why Can't I Learn Like Everyone Else?
Kids with Learning Disabilities

What's Wrong with My Brain?
Kids with Brain Injury

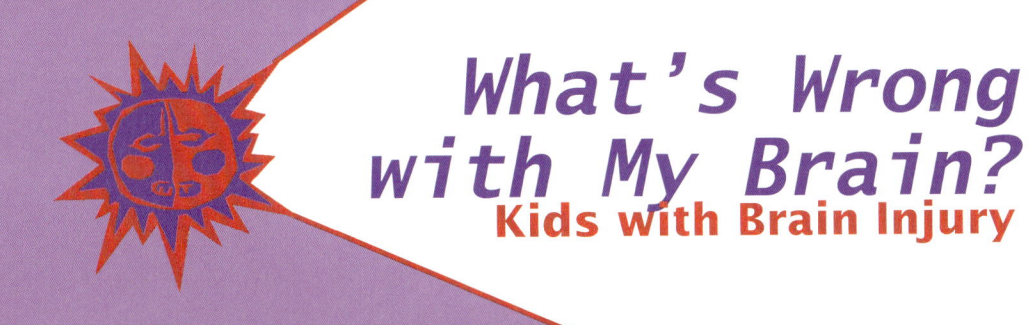

by Sheila Stewart and Camden Flath

Copyright © 2011 by Mason Crest Publishers. All rights reserved. No part of this publication may be reproduced or transmitted in any form or by any means, electronic or mechanical, including photocopying, recording, taping, or any information storage and retrieval system, without permission from the publisher.

MASON CREST PUBLISHERS INC.
370 Reed Road
Broomall, Pennsylvania 19008
(866)MCP-BOOK (toll free)
www.masoncrest.com

First Printing
9 8 7 6 5 4 3 2 1

ISBN (set) 978-1-4222-1727-6   ISBN (pbk set) 978-1-4222-1918-8

Library of Congress Cataloging-in-Publication Data

Stewart, Sheila, 1975–
  What's wrong with my brain? : kids with brain injury / by Sheila Stewart and Camden Flath.
      p. cm.
  Includes bibliographical references and index.
  ISBN 978-1-4222-1725-2   ISBN (pbk) 978-1-4222-1928-7
  1. Brain-damaged children—Juvenile literature. I. Flath, Camden, 1987– II. Title.
  RJ496.B7S74 2010
  618.92'8—dc22
                          2010010011

Produced by Harding House Publishing Service, Inc.
www.hardinghousepages.com
Design by MK Bassett-Harvey.
Cover design by Torque Advertising Design.
Printed in the USA by Bang Printing.

Photo Credits
Creative Commons Attribution 2.0 Generic: Divine in the Daily: pg. 43, WellspringCS: pg. 40; GNU Free Documentation License, Version 1.2

The creators of this book have made every effort to provide accurate information, but it should not be used as a substitute for the help and services of trained professionals.

Introduction

To the Teacher

Kids with Special Needs provides a unique forum for demystifying a wide variety of childhood medical and developmental disabilities. Written to captivate an elementary-level audience, the books bring to life the challenges and triumphs experienced by children with common chronic conditions such as hearing loss, intellectual disability, physical differences, and speech difficulties. The topics are addressed frankly through a blend of fiction and fact.

This series is particularly important today as the number of children with special needs is on the rise. Over the last two decades, advances in pediatric medical techniques have allowed children who have chronic illnesses and disabilities to live longer, more functional lives. At the same time, IDEA, a federal law, guarantees their rights to equal educational opportunities. As a result, these children represent an increasingly visible part of North American population in all aspects of daily life. Students are exposed to peers with special needs in their classrooms, through extracurricular activities, and in the community. Often, young people have misperceptions and unanswered questions about a child's disabilities—and more important, his or her abilities. Many times, there is no vehicle for talking about these complex issues in a comfortable manner.

This series will encourage further conversation about these issues. Most important, the series promotes a greater comfort for its readers as they live, play, and study side by side with these children who have medical and developmental differences—kids with special needs.

—Dr. Carolyn Bridgemohan
Boston Pediatric Hospital/Harvard Medical School

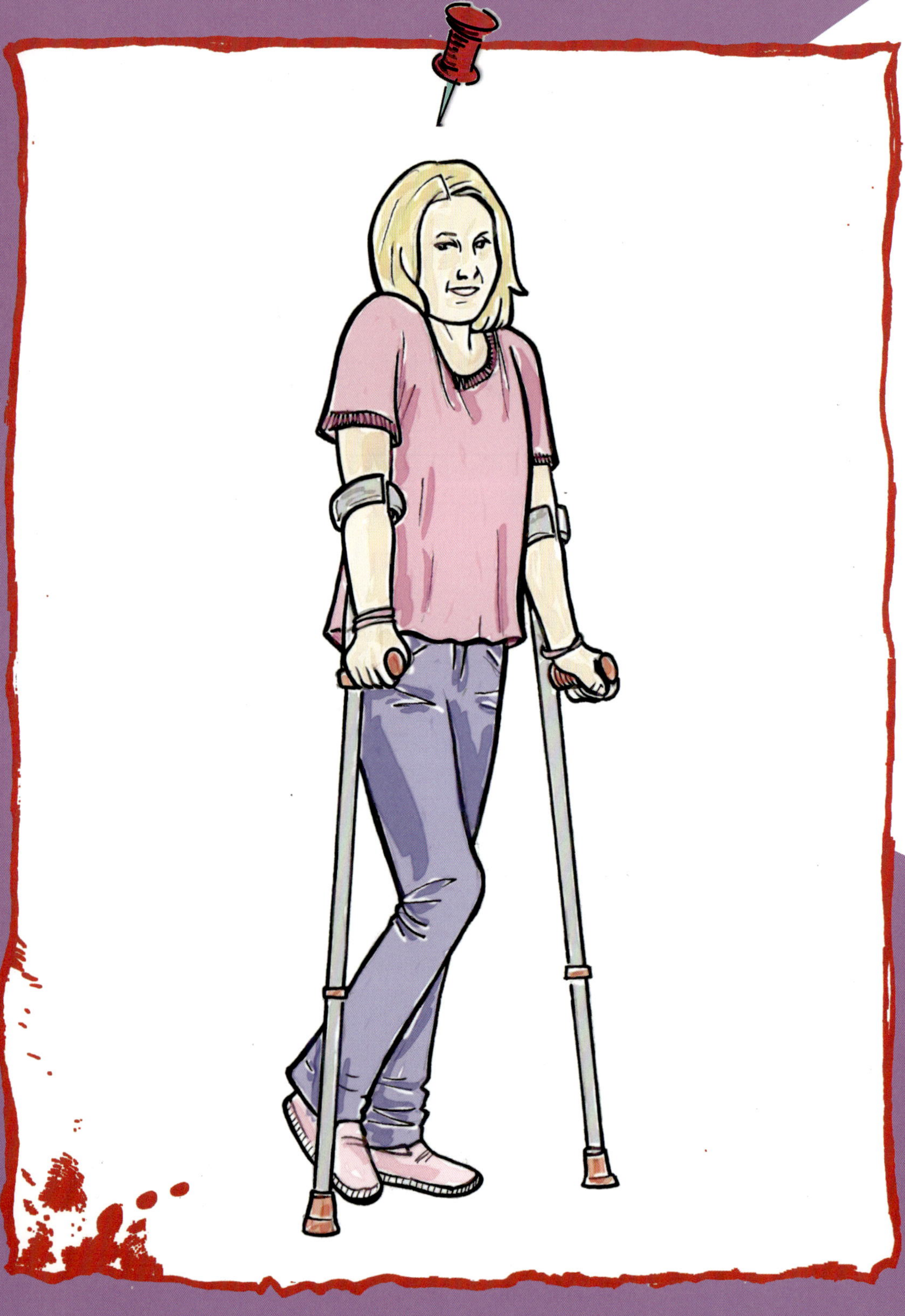

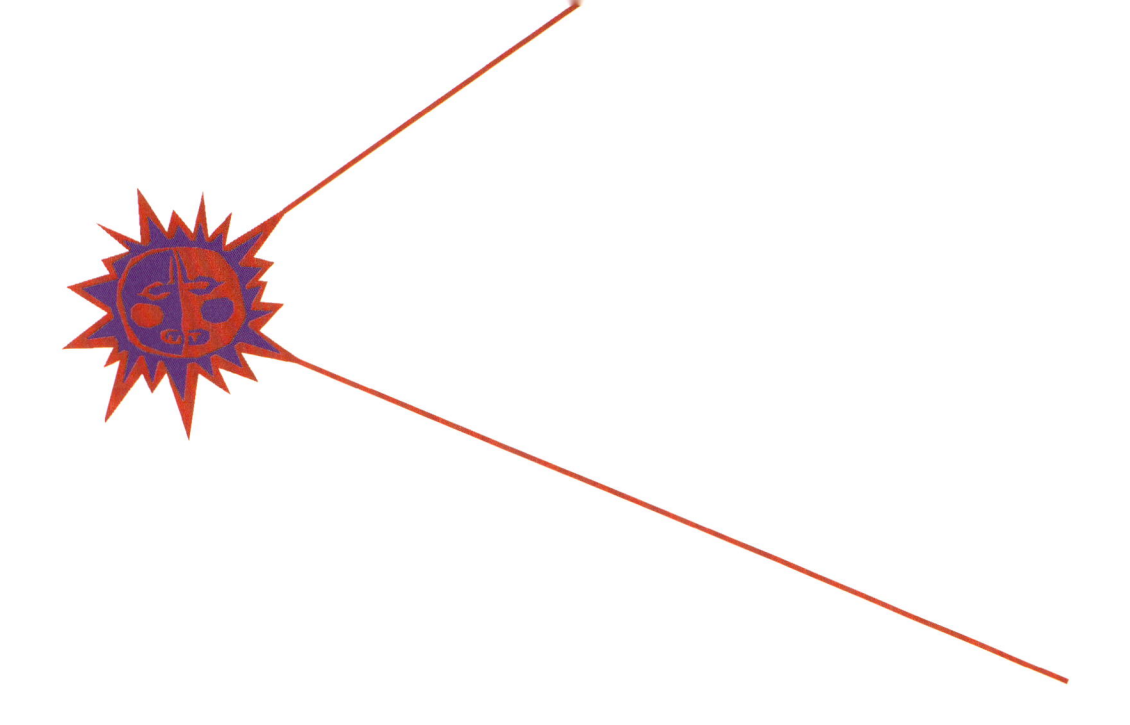

Grace gripped the handles of her forearm crutches as she shuffled up the wheelchair ramp into school.

Her dad was right behind her, ready to catch her if she fell, even though she didn't want him there. She wanted to be able to run up the front steps like she used to, but instead she could barely drag her body. Her legs—along with the rest of her body—didn't want to listen to her anymore.

She hated it.

What's Wrong with My Brain?

Gavin, her six-year-old brother, had already disappeared inside the school. Ever since the accident, when she had fallen out of a tree and landed on her head, he was nervous to be around her. It was like he didn't think she was the same person anymore.

But she *was* the same person—sort of. Except that now she couldn't remember things as well and she had trouble walking and holding a pencil. Before, she had always been running and jumping and climbing trees. Of course that was what had gotten her into trouble. She didn't even remember climbing the tree, let alone falling out of it. Claudia, her thirteen-year-old sister, had told her about it, about how the branch had broken when Grace was standing on it.

It had been more than a month since the accident, but this was Grace's first day back at school. She felt like her muscles were all jittering with impatience as she struggled into the school.

She just wanted life to get back to normal.

Everybody went quiet when Grace walked into class. The room looked pretty much the same as it had the last time she'd been here, five weeks ago, but at the same time, everything was different now. Five weeks ago, she'd been normal, just one of the crowd. Now, everyone was looking at her. Even her best friends, Samantha and Alexis, stared at her. Grace hadn't seen them since the accident, although they had sent her get-well cards.

Very slowly, Grace pulled her legs and her crutches down the aisle to her desk. She was afraid she'd trip over something and fall down in a tangle.

Mrs. Childe had been doing something at her desk when Grace came in, but now she looked up. "Grace!" she said. "Welcome back! We've missed you!"

Grace fell into her seat. She tried to get her crutches off her arms and lay them down beside her. They clattered against the floor, and she felt the eyes of the whole class watching her. She was exhausted, just from walking into class, and she was a little

10   *What's Wrong with My Brain?*

dizzy, too. Her eyes went blurry for a minute, but she blinked, and slowly her vision cleared.

Mrs. Childe told everybody to take out their journals and write in them for fifteen minutes. They did this every morning. Grace looked down at her last entry. She had written about Samantha's birthday party and sleepover, and how much she was looking forward to it. She remembered writing that. She hadn't been able to go to the party, though.

Grace picked up her pencil. Her fingers wouldn't wrap around the pencil the right way, though. She held it in her fist and tried to write. "I am back," she wrote across the page. The letters were big and sloppy, but she could read them. Maybe they were a beginning.

By lunchtime, Grace was exhausted and just wanted to take a nap. When her class went the cafeteria, Grace stayed at the end of the line. She hooked her lunch bag over the handle of one of the crutches.

"How are you doing?" someone asked.

Grace turned and saw Ms. Sanchez, the teacher's aide. Ms. Sanchez was young, with long black hair and a kind smile. Grace had always liked her.

"I'm okay." She wished her voice was clearer, but it had sounded thick and blurry since the accident.

"Let me know if you need anything," Ms. Sanchez said. "There are a lot of people at this school who want to do everything they can to help you succeed."

Grace knew that. Before she had come back to school, her dad had gone to a meeting here. He and a bunch of other people had talked about what kind of special help Grace would need when she came back. Grace didn't want any special help. She wanted to go back to being normal and just needing the same regular help as her friends. Her dad had explained to her that all these different people—the physical therapist and the occupational therapist and the speech therapist—along with her teachers, were going to do everything they could to help her get back to normal, even though it would probably take a very long time and she might never be exactly the same. She hadn't wanted to hear that.

He had looked her in the eyes and said, "I'm never going to lie to you, Grace. It's not going to be easy, but you're not in this alone."

Grace felt tears in her eyes as she remembered, but she made herself smile back at Ms. Sanchez.

Grace found Samantha and Alexis in the cafeteria. She went over and sat with them. They glanced at each other and then at her.

"Hey," Alexis said. "How's it going?"

It was a normal question, but something about the way she said it made Grace feel weird, like Alexis didn't want to talk about what had happened to Grace. But then, wasn't that exactly what Grace wanted? To be treated normally?

"Hey." She smiled at them and tried to make her voice sound normal. "So, what have I missed while I've been gone?"

Samantha looked uncertain for a moment. "My party was good," she said. "And Joey's parents let him have a real dance party. The whole class came—well, except for you—and they had a DJ and a disco ball. It was great!"

Grace didn't think that was the kind of thing she had wanted to know. But, then again, she didn't know what she *had* meant when she asked the question.

"Oh," she said.

Alexis glared at Samantha. "We learned about the American Revolution in history," she said. "And we learned about photosynthesis in science."

"Oh," Grace said again. She wasn't sure she had meant that either.

But at least they were trying.

After lunch, Grace's class had computer and then gym, while Grace had therapy and then more therapy. She had physical therapy first. The physical therapist's name was Maggie, and she reminded Grace a little of her dad's girlfriend, Amy.

Kids with Brain Injury 15

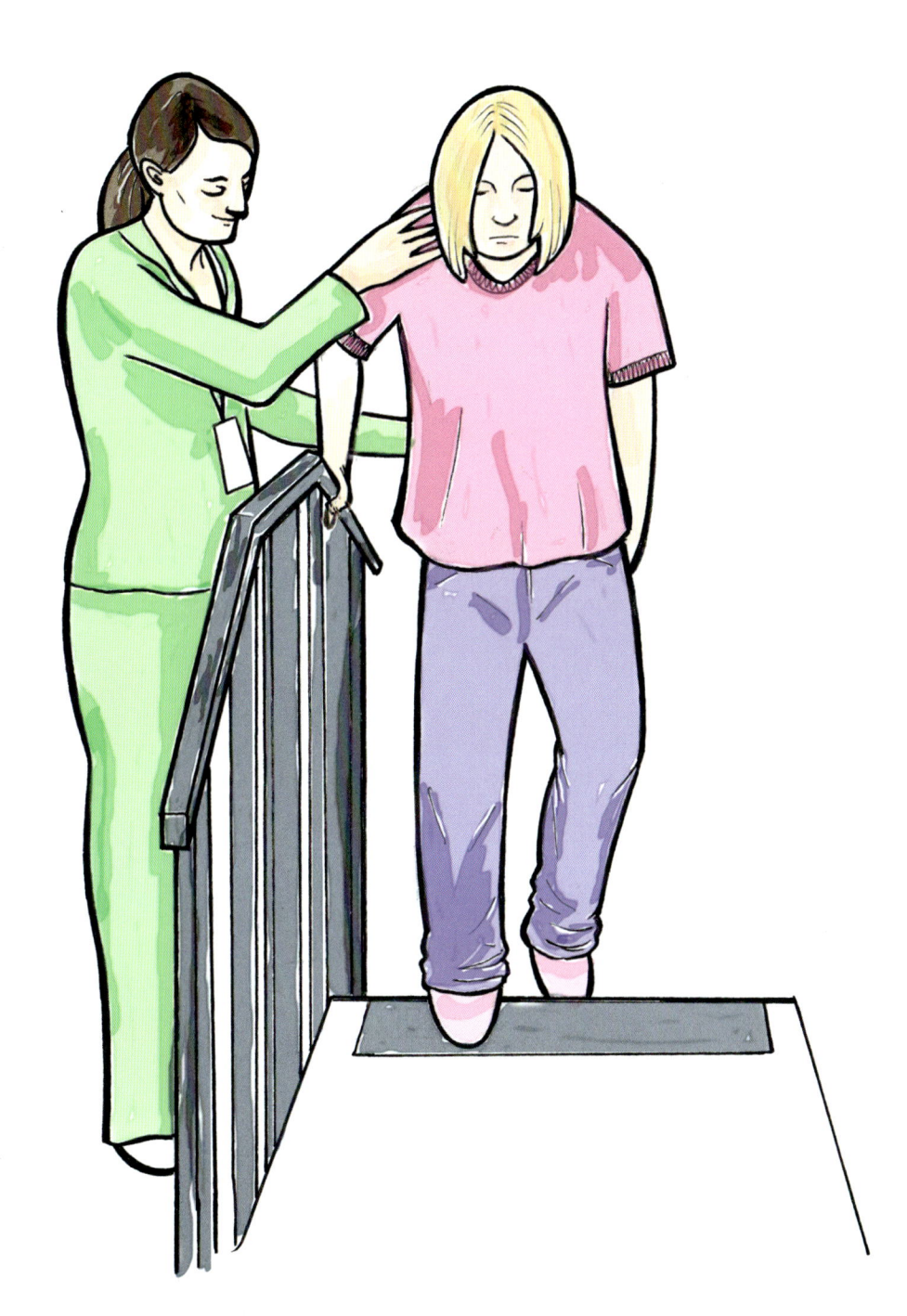

"Okay, Grace," Maggie said. "I know you've been doing physical therapy at home, and what we'll be doing here will be very similar. We'll be working to build up your leg strength and improve your walking skills."

She helped Grace stretch the muscles in her legs, and then they worked on walking and climbing stairs. At first, Grace used her crutches, but by the end of the session, Maggie had her walking without them, holding on to the stair railings. That was hard, but Grace was excited that she'd been able to do it without falling down.

It had also been very tiring—and Grace had already been tired. Maggie brought her some water and a granola bar, and then the session was over. Now it was time for occupational therapy. At least she didn't have speech therapy today too.

The occupational therapist introduced herself as "Miss Kate." She was about the same age as Maggie, but she wasn't quite as nice and smiley.

"Let's get started with those fingers," she said briskly.

She had Grace start picking up marbles one at a time, moving them from one bowl to another. Grace's fingers didn't want to cooperate, and she kept dropping the marbles so they went rolling across the table or the floor.

"I can't do this." Grace was near tears.

"Yes, you can," Miss Kate said. "Keep going."

So Grace rubbed the tears out of her eyes with the back of her hand and kept going.

After occupational therapy, Miss Kate walked Grace back to her classroom. She got there just before the other kids got back from gym, so she was able to sit down and get her crutches arranged before everyone else came in.

The next class was math. Grace had always been good at math. But now, along with everything else that had changed since the accident, that didn't seem to

18 *What's Wrong with My Brain?*

be true anymore. The class was working on changing fractions into decimals. She felt like she couldn't make her brain even think about the numbers. She tried to take deep breaths and force herself to focus.

The fraction that Mrs. Childe had written on the board was four over nine.

"So," Mrs. Childe said, "we need to divide four by nine in order to find the decimal."

She wrote the equation on the board and solved it. There seemed to be a lot of zeros and fours, and the equation trailed down the board as a line of fours ran out sideways. Grace had no idea what Mrs. Childe was talking about.

Mrs. Childe started another problem on the board. "What's four times eight?" she asked the class, although Grace didn't know why she was asking this particular question.

Half the class raised their hands to answer the question. Grace thought about it. She remembered learning the multiplication tables years ago. She had known them all; they had been easy. But now she had no idea what the answer was.

"Thirty-two," somebody said, and the answer didn't even sound familiar.

She put her head down on her desk and started to cry.

Somebody touched her shoulder.

"Grace, are you okay?" Ms. Sanchez asked quietly.

Grace rubbed her eyes, but the tears kept coming. She looked up and saw that, once again, everyone was staring at her.

"I want to go home," she said to Ms. Sanchez.

Ms. Sanchez didn't argue with her. She handed Grace her crutches and helped her stand up. Grace made her way up the aisle between the desks, trying to pretend that people weren't staring at her, that tears weren't still running down her cheeks.

Out in the hallway, she leaned against the wall and tried to breathe normally.

"There's only about half an hour left before school ends," Ms. Sanchez said. "You can wait in the nurse's office."

That wasn't what Grace wanted. She wanted everything to be right again. She wanted to be able to walk again and understand math like she used to.

But the nurse's office would be better than going back into class.

"Why don't I go back and get your backpack?" Ms. Sanchez suggested, and Grace nodded.

When Ms. Sanchez had gone back inside the room, Grace decided to start walking to the nurse's office. She felt like she needed to move, to *do* something.

She was halfway down the hall when she realized she couldn't remember where the nurse's office was.

She looked up and down the hallway. None of it looked familiar at all, which made her more frustrated and scared. She'd gone to this school since she was in kindergarten.

She'd forgotten that Ms. Sanchez would be back in a few minutes with her backpack. Would her feet remember the way to go, even if her brain didn't? She started walking again.

Another hallway branched off to the right. Grace hesitated. The other hallway was short, and turned at the end. She decided it looked promising and went that way.

At the end of the short hallway, Grace turned right. She didn't have a real reason for going that way. She just felt like it. The hall ended with a doorway. She opened the door and looked inside. The room was full of little kids wearing art smocks and holding paintbrushes. She closed the door before they could notice her.

She started trying doors along the hall, opening them a crack and looking inside. She found the computer room, a janitor's closet, and the library, but still no nurse's office. She was getting frustrated, but she was still determined.

Kids with Brain Injury 23

Suddenly one of her crutches slipped. She felt herself falling, and one hand went out to catch herself. With her other hand, she tried to protect her head. The doctor had told her that hitting her head again could hurt her brain even worse.

She landed in a heap on the floor, but she wasn't hurt. She was mad, though. Really mad. She screamed and threw her crutches, one after the other across the hall, and then she was even angrier that they didn't go very far.

Ms. Sanchez was out of breath as she came around the corner carrying Grace's backpack. "Are you okay? I heard you scream."

"I fell down." The anger was starting to go away and she just felt tired again. And sad.

Ms. Sanchez picked up the crutches and helped Grace get up. Then she led her back to the first hallway and then further down that to the nurse's office.

"Grace is just going to sit here until her dad comes," Ms. Sanchez said to the nurse. Then Ms. Sanchez turned back to Grace. "Do you want to talk about what happened in class?"

Grace was quiet for a moment, then she said, "I just don't know how to do it anymore. It used to be easy and now everything is just . . . just . . . gone."

"This has been a hard day for you, hasn't it?" Ms. Sanchez ran her hand over Grace's hair. "It's a lot to handle for your first day back. It will get easier, I think. We have an intern who is going to come and work with you one-on-one in math. He'll start tomorrow. Did your dad tell you about that?"

Grace didn't know if he'd told her or not. He might have and she'd just forgotten. For a moment, she was both relieved about having someone to help her and upset that she needed help, but then she made herself focus on the relief. Things weren't going to go back to the way they were just because she wished they could.

Grace's dad arrived just after the bell rang.

"How did it go?" He looked nervous and hopeful.

"I survived," Grace said. "That's got to count for something."

He smiled and hugged her. "Yep, it counts," he said. "Let's get Gavin and then we'll go pick up Claudia. I thought we could get a pizza and eat it in the living room. We'll celebrate your first day back at school. Amy's coming over too."

"Really? The living room?" Grace started to smile a little. "That's pretty extreme."

"You're an extreme kid." He helped her stand up and took her backpack for her.

Later, at home, Grace started to relax finally.

"How'd it go?" Claudia asked her.

"Weird," said Grace. "I didn't like everyone staring at me. Then I got lost. . . ."

"Wow," Claudia said. "Yeah, I guess that would be pretty weird." She hesitated, then she said, "Listen, I know things have been kind of weird between you and me, too, lately. I think I felt like it was my fault that you fell, like I should have done something to protect you. I'm your big sister, after all."

"Really?" Grace asked. "But it wasn't your fault at all."

"But I love you," Claudia said. "I hate it that you got hurt."

"Me too," said Gavin, unexpectedly.

"We all love you," said Amy.

Her dad smiled and winked at her.

And for at least the fourth time that day, Grace felt tears in her eyes, but these were better tears. She felt like no matter how hard it was going to be, things would get better.

Kids and Brain Injury

When a brain is hurt, it can change the way a person thinks, talks, and gets along with others. Kids who have a *traumatic* brain injury may have physical difficulties as well. They may not be able to walk, move, and play the way other kids do. Because the brain is so important to who we are and what we do, a traumatic brain injury can change a person's life in many ways.

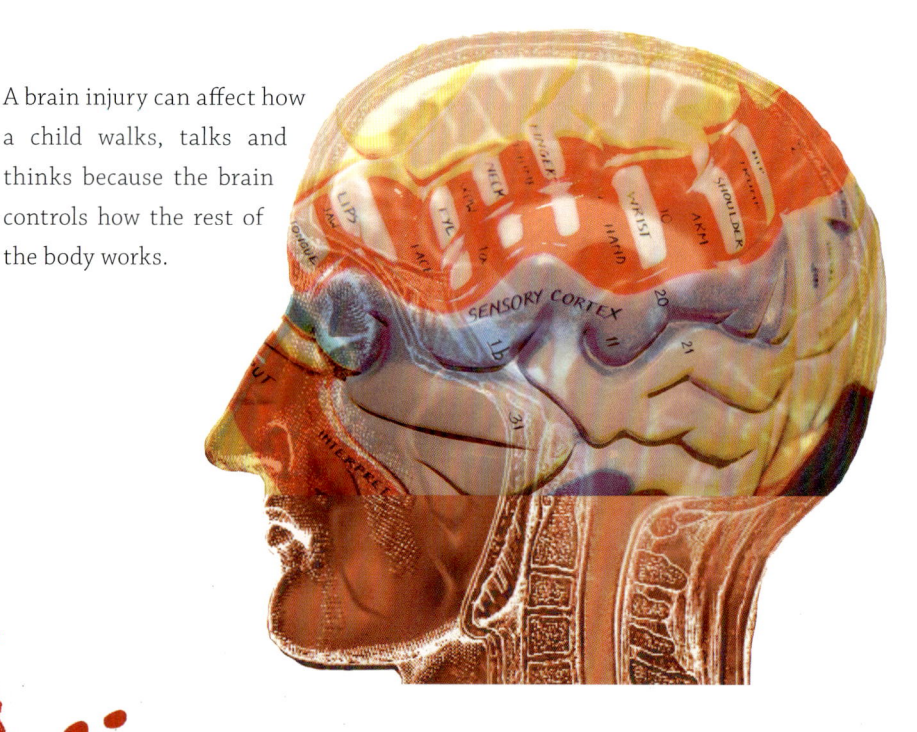

Traumatic means that something causes hurts or shocks your body very much.

A brain injury can affect how a child walks, talks and thinks because the brain controls how the rest of the body works.

Sometimes called TBI, traumatic brain injury is an injury that damages the brain. Traumatic brain injuries are different from other injuries. While a cut may heal, or a broken bone may be put into a cast until the bone grows back together, an injury to a person's brain can change the way that person thinks or acts forever. Kids with this kind of injury may have trouble playing with other kids, making friends, or paying attention in school. They may not be able to do things they once were able to do, like hold a pencil, remember simple facts, or tie their shoes. A traumatic brain injury can even change someone's **personality** as well as cause other **disabilities** and medical risks. The person may look the same—but inside, his brain is not the same. He is faced with a whole new world, filled with things he used to be able to do that he must now learn to do all over again. It can be both frightening and frustrating.

> Your **personality** is all the things that make you different from anyone else—the way you act, the way you think, all your traits and characteristics.
>
> **Disabilities** are problems—either physical or mental—that get in the way of a person doing what other people can do.

The Effects of Traumatic Brain Injury

The kinds of things that are hard for a kid to do after this kind of injury will depend on the part of the brain that was hurt. Different parts of the brain control different things. So if a child injures the part of the brain used during speech, she will have a hard time talking. If another child injures the part of the brain that controls emotions, she may have a hard time with her moods.

> *Social* has to do with getting along with other people.
>
> *Physical* has to do with your body.
>
> If someone is *paralyzed*, she cannot move all or part of her body.

Kids with brain injuries may have one or all of the following three types of problems:

- *Social* difficulties: Kids with brain injuries may have difficulty understanding others, controlling their emotions, and telling others how they feel. They may also have sudden mood changes.
- *Physical* disabilities: Kids with brain injuries might have a hard time speaking, walking, or writing. Some people who have brain injuries may be *paralyzed* on one or both sides of their bodies.

- **Intellectual** *difficulties*: A brain injury can make it harder for child to learn, understand, pay attention, solve problems, and remember. A kid with a traumatic brain injury may not be able to pay attention for long periods of time. He might not be able to remember things he was just told. Making up his mind or thinking through a decision quickly may be hard for him to do.

> **Intellectual** has to do with your mind and your ability to think and learn.

A child with a traumatic brain injury may have trouble in school because she is not able to learn as easily as other children, or because she has trouble in social situations.

The Causes of Traumatic Brain Injury

Brain injuries can happen during a car crash. They can also happen when kids are playing sports. Any kind of accident where a person hits his head can cause a traumatic brain injury if the blow is hard enough. The most common causes of head injury are car crashes, guns, and falls.

There are two main types of head injury that can damage the brain:

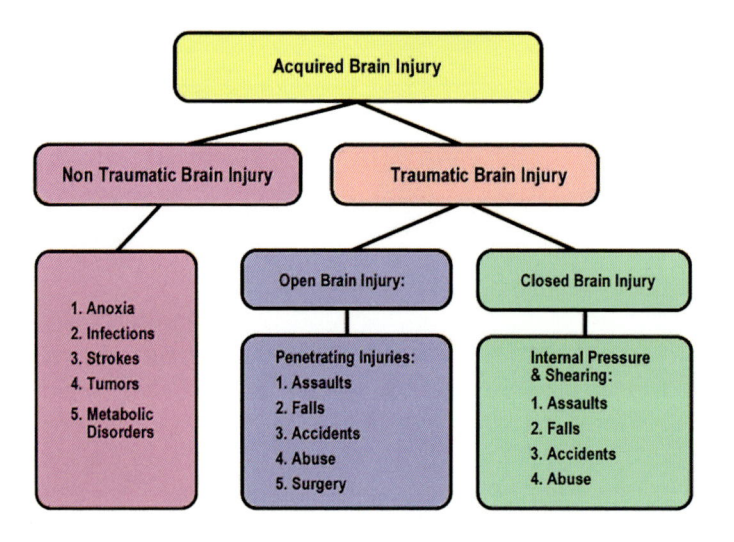

```
                    Acquired Brain Injury
                    /                   \
        Non Traumatic Brain Injury    Traumatic Brain Injury
                                      /                \
                              Open Brain Injury:    Closed Brain Injury
        1. Anoxia
        2. Infections             Penetrating         Internal Pressure
        3. Strokes                Injuries:           & Shearing:
        4. Tumors                 1. Assaults         1. Assaults
        5. Metabolic              2. Falls            2. Falls
           Disorders              3. Accidents        3. Accidents
                                  4. Abuse            4. Abuse
                                  5. Surgery
```

This chart describes the different types of brain injury. Non traumatic brain injuries are those injuries caused by illnesses, while traumatic brain injuries are caused by accidents or other blows to the head.

- *Open-head injury*: An open-head injury is one that breaks through the skull and damages a specific part of the brain. Gunshots, stabbings, and other injuries that **puncture** the head are open-head injuries. These injuries are sometimes called **penetrating**-head injuries.

> To **puncture** means to pierce or poke a hole in something.
>
> **Penetrating** means poking or pushing through something.

- *Closed-head injury*: A closed-head injury is one that does not break through the skull. Hitting the head during a fall or accident, for example, might damage the brain but not break through the skull.

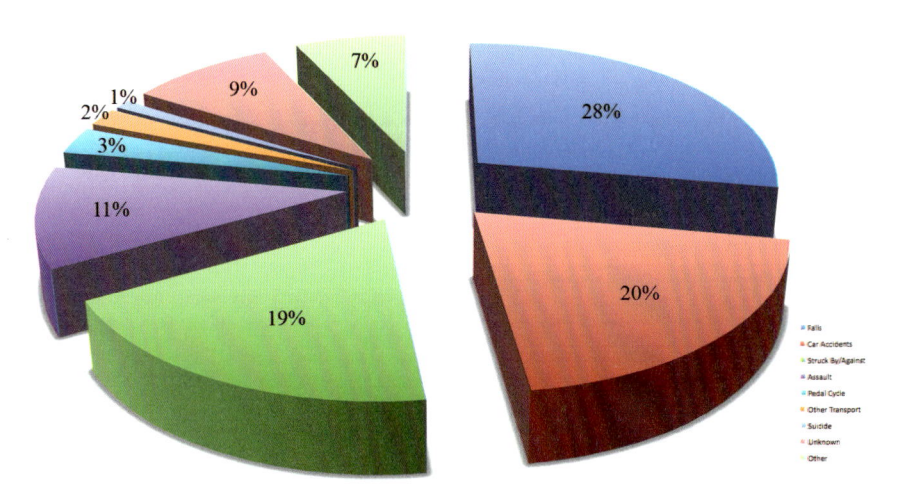

This chart shows the most common causes of traumatic brain injury. For children age 0 to 4 years, falls are the leading cause of brain injury, while car accidents are the most common cause of brain injuries for adolescents age 15 to 19 years.

Not every injury to the head damages the brain—and not every traumatic brain injury is caused by a person hitting his head. Other causes of traumatic brain injury include:

- *Infection*: An infection in the brain can cause permanent damage.
- *Chemicals/poisons*: Some brain injuries can be caused by chemicals. **Lead** poisoning and **carbon monoxide** poisoning are two examples. Certain **pesticides** can also cause damage to the brain.
- *Lack of oxygen*: If the brain does not get enough oxygen, or gets no oxygen, for a long enough period of time, the brain can be permanently damaged. This might happen during a swimming accident, for instance.

> **Lead** *is a metal found in old paints and old pipes that can damage the brain if it is swallowed.*
>
> **Carbon monoxide** *is a colorless, odorless gas that can prevent your body from getting oxygen when you breathe.*
>
> **Pesticides** *are chemicals used to kill insects.*

Diagnosing Traumatic Brain Injury

After a child injures her head, doctors must first find out how serious the injury is. Doctors use three categories to *diagnose* different levels of traumatic brain injury. These ratings are based on how long a person is unconscious or in a *coma* after being injured. The three main types of traumatic brain injury are:

- *Mild TBI*: less than one hour of coma, short loss of consciousness or no loss of consciousness.
- *Moderate TBI*: a coma lasting less than twenty-four hours.
- *Severe TBI*: a coma lasting longer than twenty-four hours.

> To *diagnose* means to figure out what is wrong with someone. Usually, a doctor is the person who makes a diagnosis.
>
> A *coma* is a long period of very deep unconsciousness.
>
> *Moderate* means that something is in the middle—not a lot, not a little.
>
> *Severe* means that something is very serious or bad.

The effects of a mild TBI may not be seen for some time after the injury. This can make diagnosing mild TBI more difficult than moderate or severe TBI.

When doctors think that a patient might have some form of brain injury, they can do several tests to check for damage in the brain. A CAT scan, for instance, is a machine that doctors use to take pictures of the brain. Using this technology, they can see any bleeding, swelling, or damage. An expert in the way that the brain works, a neurologist, can recognize damage in the brain and explain its effects.

Treating Traumatic Brain Injury

After a child has been treated at the hospital for a head injury, he will probably need treatment for the long-term

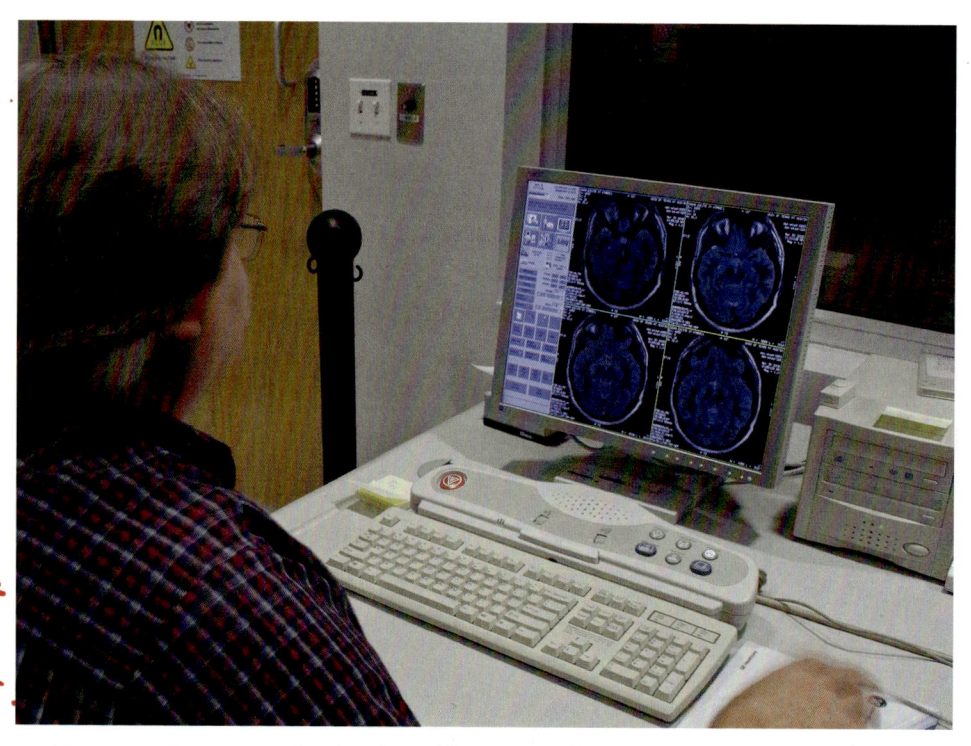

Doctors can use special technology, like an MRI or CAT scan, to check the brain for injury. This doctor is reading brain scan images on a computer.

problems caused by his injury. Although there is no cure for these long-term problems, a child with this type of injury can be taught how to cope with these problems and learn better ways to live with them.

Rehabilitation *is a way of getting a person as much back to normal as possible after an injury.*

One of the most common treatments is called **rehabilitation** or rehab. The main goal of rehab is to help a child with brain injury learn to function in school and at home as best as she can. Different in-

A child with brain injury may have to undergo rehabilitation to help her with walking or talking. This girl rides a horse once a week, which helps her strengthen her legs to improve her walking ability.

37

juries will need different types of treatment and ***therapy*** in rehabilitation. A kid with mild TBI may only need help with classroom skills like memory or clear speech. Someone with moderate or severe TBI might need more help with moving, walking, or speaking. Rehabilitation can be done at home, where ***therapists*** will come to visit,

> **Therapy** *is the treatment of disease or injury. It's a way to help a person get better.*
>
> **Therapists** *are people who are specially trained to do therapy.*

Therapists, like the one shown here, may work with a child in an office, but they may also visit the child at home or at school.

38

or in a hospital or school. Experts in speech, language, thinking, movement, and social skills can help kids work on many different skills.

Many kids with brain injury will also need to be watched over for any medical problems. Rehabilitation programs usually have doctors on hand who are experts in brain injury.

Traumatic Brain Injury and School

Going back to school can be very hard for a child with a brain injury. Kids with brain injury may not have the skills they did before they were injured. Memory, thought, movement, speech, and learning may all be different, so kids with these kinds of injuries will need to be *evaluated* to see what they can and can't do.

*When something is **evaluated**, it is examined to see in which category it belongs.*

Special education *teaches kids who have trouble learning because of some disability.*

Some children with brain injury will need *special education*. A law called the Individuals with Disabilities Education Act (IDEA) outlines how schools should decide which kids need special education.

If a child's brain injury affects his education, the IDEA law requires that he receive a specialized education plan to help him succeed.

In order to **qualify** for special education under IDEA, the child's brain injury must get in the way of her learning or taking part in school activities.

The IDEA law lists thirteen different kinds of disabilities that may mean a child will qualify for special education. Traumatic brain injury is one **category** under the law.

> To **qualify** means to fit the definition of something or to meet the requirements.
>
> A **category** is a group or a certain kind of thing.

40

The IDEA law requires that:

- the child has problems performing well at school activities.
- the child's parent, teacher, or other school staff person must ask that the child be examined for a disability.
- the child is evaluated to decide if she does indeed have a disability and to figure out what kind of special education she needs.
- a group of people, including the kid's parents, teachers, and a school psychologist, meets to decide on a plan for helping him. This plan is called an Individualized Education Program (IEP). The IEP spells out exactly what the child needs in order to succeed at school. Speech therapy, *physical therapy*, or *occupational therapy* might all be parts of the IEP for a child with a brain injury, along with class work and lessons that are matched to his abilities.

> *Physical therapy helps a kid learn how to move around again, the way she did before a brain injury.*
>
> *Occupational therapy teaches a child with brain injury how to do the things he needs to do for daily life, such as tie his shoes, write with a pen or pencil, or brush his teeth.*

Preventing Traumatic Brain Injury

People with brain injury can learn how to live again—but brain injuries don't have to happen. You can prevent a brain injury by:

- *Wearing a helmet*: Wearing a helmet when playing sports (especially contact sports like football or boxing) or riding a bike, or while skateboarding or skiing is the best way to prevent head injury.
- *Gun safety*: Never treat guns like toys. Never even handle a gun unless you're with an adult who knows about guns.
- *Car safety*: Wearing your seatbelt can protect you from a head injury during a crash or sudden stop. Also, never ride in a car driven by someone who has used alcohol or drugs.

Succeeding with Brain Injury

Traumatic brain injury can change a kid's life in a moment. Many kids who have these injuries may need help for the rest of their lives from their parents, from their brothers and sisters, and from teachers and therapists. Kids with brain injuries face many **challenges** that others may not.

> **Challenges** are things you find difficult.

Many kids succeed in spite of these challenges, and go on to do great things. Although brain injuries do not go

Safety devices, like bike helmets or car seat belts, can help prevent traumatic brain injury.

away, most kids will learn to cope with them. Some will slowly relearn many of the skills that the injury took away from them. Others may have to face certain challenges for the rest of their lives.

If someone you know has had a brain injury, you can make her life harder by teasing her and treating her differently—or you can help her put her life back together a little more quickly by being her friend!

Further Reading

Cassidy, J. W. and L. Woodruff. *Mindstorms: Living with Traumatic Brain Injury.* Cambridge, Mass.: Da Capo Press, 2009.

Crimmins, C. *Where is the Mango Princess? A Journey Back from Brain Injury.* New York: Vintage Books, 2000.

Jameson, Larry and Beth Jameson. *Brain Injury Survivor's Guide: Welcome to Our World.* Parker, Colo.: Outskirts Press, 2007.

Mason, M. P. *Head Cases: Stories of Brain Injury and Its Aftermath.* New York: Farrar, Straus, and Giroux, 2008.

Senelick, R. C. *Living with Brain Injury: A Guide for Families.* Florence, Ken.: Cengage Learning, 2001.

Taylor, Laura. *For Kids Only: A Kid's Guide to Brain Injury.* Richmond, Va.: National Resource Center on Traumatic Brain Injury, 2003.

Find Out More On the Internet

Brain Injury Association of America, Inc.
www.biausa.org

Brain Trauma Foundation
www.braintrauma.org

Centre for Neuro Skills TBI Resource Guide
www.neuroskills.com

Head Injury Hotline and Brain Injury Resource Center
www.headinjury.com

International Brain Injury Association
www.internationalbrain.org

The National Dissemination Center for Children with Disabilities (NICHCY)
www.nichcy.org

National Institute of Neurological Disorders and Stroke (NINDS): Traumatic Brain Injury Information Page
www.ninds.nih.gov/disorders/tbi/tbi.htm

TBI (Traumatic Brain Injury Information)
traumatic-brain-injury.net

TraumaticBrainInjury.com
www.traumaticbraininjury.com

Disclaimer

The websites listed on this page were active at the time of publication. The publisher is not responsible for websites that have changed their address or discontinued operation since the date of publication. The publisher will review and update the websites upon each reprint.

Index

alcohol 42

car 32, 42
carbon monoxide 34
CAT scan 35
challenges 42, 44
classroom 38
closed-head injury 33
coma 35

diagnose 35

emotions 30

gun 32, 33, 42

Individualized Education
 Program (IEP) 41
Individuals with Disabilities
 Education Act (IDEA) 39–41
infection 34
intellectual 31

lead 34

medical risks 29

neurologist 36

occupational therapy 41
open-head injury 33

paralyzed 30
penetrating 33
personality 29
pesticides 34
physical therapy 41
puncture 33

qualify 40

rehabilitation 37–39

social 30, 39
special education 39–41

therapy 38, 41
traumatic 28-32, 34, 35, 37, 39,
 40, 42
traumatic brain injury (TBI)
 28–35, 37, 38, 42

About the Authors

Sheila Stewart has written several dozen books for young people, both fiction and nonfiction, although she especially enjoys writing fiction. She has a master's degree in English and now works as a writer and editor. She lives with her two children in a house overflowing with books, in the Southern Tier of New York State.

Camden Flath is a writer living and working in Binghamton, New York. He has a degree in English and has written several books for young people. He is interested in current political, social, and economic issues and applies those interests to his writing.

About the Consultant

Dr. Carolyn Bridgemohan is board certified in developmental behavioral pediatrics and practices at the Developmental Medicine Center at Children's Hospital Boston. She is the director of the Autism Care Program and an assistant professor at Harvard Medical School. Her specialty areas are autism and other pervasive developmental disorders, developmental and learning problems, and developmental and behavioral pediatrics.